Amazon FBA for Beginners

A Step-By-Step Guide on Fulfilment By Amazon

Table of Contents

Introduction 1

Chapter One: What is FBA? 3

Chapter Two: How to Sign Up on Amazon FBA to
Get Started 9

Chapter Three: How to Find a Profitable Product
That Will Sell 13

Chapter Four: How to Ship and Manage Inventory 25

Chapter Five: How to Market for Improving Sales 35

Chapter Six: How to Get Stellar Reviews Every Time 39

Chapter Seven: Learning About Fees and Tax Issues 45

Conclusion 55

Introduction

Are you exhausted from of your nine to five desk job? Perhaps you are looking for a way to become financially stable. What if we told you that there is now a way to do this, from your own home? Luckily, you have decided to come to the right book! In the chapters to follow, we will be providing you with all of the techniques and strategies you will need to become successful on FBA.

As you will be learning in the first chapter, FBA stands for Fulfilment by Amazon. This is a new medium for online sales. By learning everything you need to know about the program, you will skip over the learning curve of figuring out a new site. Whether you are a new to the internet era or an all time expert, this step-by-step guide is for absolutely anyone! This is why we will first be going over what FBA is. This way, you can decide if this is the program for you or not.

In our second chapter, we will give you a step-by-step guide to get you signed up for Amazon FBA. Sometimes, it can be a bit tricky, but we will give you the tools you need to get started. By being prepared, you will be able to jump into the game and make money as soon as possible! The initial question you should be asking yourself is, what am I going to sell? We can help out with that too.

In this book, we will be saving you the time of choosing out your product. We have done all of the research you need to find out what is hot on the market. Sure, you could sell something you are passionate about, or you could sell

Introduction

something that will bring in the dough quickly. We suggest finding a good in-between. After all, you never want to hate what you are handling. If you do, you probably will not stick with FBA. Luckily, there is a lot of real money from internet sales. Yes, you will have to work for it; but it will be worth it once you learn the ropes.

Once you have decided on your product, it will be time to find out how to ship your items. Hopefully, as you grow, you will have clients all over the world! Thanks to Amazon, this isn't as difficult as it sounds. You will be learning more about that later. With shipping comes the inventory management. With modern technology, this is easier than ever. As you learn, you can choose which management method is best for your lifestyle then go from there.

Now that you have your perfect product and the ability to ship your items, it is time to get to the hard work. You need people to see your items! What you will learn is that people relations are essential to sales. In our book, we provide you with brilliant advice to improve your sales and get fantastic reviews. The more sales and reviews, the better your company looks! If you think about it, trust is a key concept in making sales. People want to feel secure in the fact that they are getting the best bang for their buck. You can make this a reality with the proper tools and knowledge of your product.

We have so much to offer within the chapters of this book. Our goal is to have you read through and feel prepared to start your own business. You deserve to be financially independent. With some hard work, anything is possible! Enjoy!

Chapter One:

What is FBA?

Let's be honest, running your business is not an easy task. Many components go into running a successful business. The question is, how is it possible to make some of these steps easier for you? This is where FBA comes into play.

FBA stands for Fulfilment By Amazon. This is an option if you wish to sell product on Amazon. While Amazon does sell its personal inventory on the website, you can get your product up on the web as well. With Fulfilment By Amazon, it takes a lot of the work out of the situation for you so your success rate increases. Below, we will provide a step-by-step guide on how this works for you.

Step One: Sending the Inventory

- This will first include the inbound quantity guidance. We will be showing you later how to ship your items in the first place.

- Amazon also offers a few optional suggestions. These include Premium placement, a prep materials store, and the choice of having an Amazon partnered carrier.

Step Two: Receive & Store the Product

- During this step, your inventory will be placed at a location that is closer to your customer.

- At this step, there are two extra options including label services and prep services.

Step Three: Customer & The Product

- At this point, customers will have open access to your product. It should be noted that there will be offers if the customer has Prime benefits. This could even include free shipping.

Step Four: Shipping the Product

- The shipping aspect is probably the most beneficial aspects of FBA. Once the customer has purchased your item, they pick up the item from their inventory, pack it up and ship it out.

Step Five: Customer Service

- Most of the time, customers are going to have questions. Whether it is about size, price, shipping information, Amazon has got you covered. They have 24/7 responses which will make your customers very happy.

Step Six: Customer Return

- Don't worry; this is bound to happen. Online sales can be tricky; this is why Amazon offers assistance with returning a product. Of course, there may be a processing fee, but the primary goal is to keep your customer happy. This will lead to your success at the end of the day.

Choosing Fulfilment By Amazon

With other markets on the internet, you may be asking yourself why you should choose FBA? If you are looking to reduce your time, increase your money, and decrease shipping time, Amazon fulfillment program is the best option for you. In fact, it comes with many benefits to the seller that you may have never considered before.

Benefit # 1: Amazon Prime

Even if you have never used FBA, you have most likely heard of Amazon Prime before. Amazon Prime is a program that usually has customers that are purchasing more items, more often compared to other Amazon shoppers. So, what does that mean exactly?

- First, Prime purchases tend to trend at an increase during the season. This means your sales will most likely go up every holiday. There was one week where around 1 million people decided to join Amazon Prime in just one week. This just goes to show you that there are a lot of customers that you are probably missing!

- Second, by using Fulfilment By Amazon, this will help increase how many of these customers see your product in the first place. On top of that, they make the deal irresistible with free shipping! You would be surprised how many people will decide not to buy a product simply due to a shipping fee. By using FBA, you increase your chances like never before.

- If you use FBA, there will more likely be a conversions table on the detail pages. This is something that is only eligible with prime. With this tool, it could also help increase your sales if you choose to go with this program.

Benefit #2- Business Operations

- As you know, running a business takes a lot of time and a lot of extra effort. Fulfillment by Amazon takes care of a majority of this. From handling and managing your product to shipping it for you, everything is taken care of without you having to give it a simple thought. You only pass your product off to Amazon and the rest is a done deal!

Benefit #3- Shipping

- As we mentioned earlier, Amazon Prime offers a quicker shipping rate. This means that your product will be processed fast and shipped out quickly. This is compared to being sent to you as a retailer. Luckily, Amazon offers amazing customer service as well, so if your customer has any questions along the way, Amazon is there too. On top of that, there is also delivery tracking. This alone is a huge perk for your customers. At the end of the day, your customer's happiness is the key to your success!

Benefit #4- All About the Brand

- Amazon is a HUGE brand name. The company has worked to be reputable and trustworthy. When your business is aligned with Amazon, your reputation increases as well. If you want to increase your sales, Amazon in 2013 stated that they were able to increase the sales of 73% of their sellers by 20% or more. If that isn't a reason to use FBA, we're not sure what is!

Benefit #5- More Sales, More Money

- As you will be learning, this is not something that will be guaranteed. Making money on Amazon FBA will require a lot of work. However, sellers have found that the volume of their sales increase when they switch to Amazon FBA. This could be altered for a number of reasons including Amazon Prime and an increased audience. For most, they found their sales doubled when they joined FBA.

If you decide to use FBA, we promise that you have made the right choice. With so many benefits, it is difficult to go wrong! Now that you understand what Fulfilment By Amazon is and all of the amazing benefits, it is time to get to the good stuff! In the next chapter, we will be providing you a step-by-step guide to get you set up on Amazon FBA so you can start making money!

Chapter Two:

How to Sign Up on Amazon FBA to Get Started

Congratulations on deciding to sign up for Amazon FBA! Your first step is to set up the accounts you will need to get your company on Amazon! This will be your very first step to success. If you ever feel confused, don't hesitate to go back and go over some of the details we have provided. Our goal is to make this step-by-step guide as easy as possible for our readers. Here is step number one!

1. New Email

    Yes, you may have a current email address that you like, but we suggest starting a new one. When you do this, it will grant easy organization for handling your new income stream. You can use whichever email provider you enjoy. We suggest using Gmail as it offers other useful tools you may enjoy using.

    As you are naming your new email ID, try to choose a name that will be close to the title of your store. If you haven't gotten this far yet, we suggest taking a quick trip over to Amazon. You can see what other retailers are calling themselves and come up with your own, unique name. Please note that this is not extremely important. It is something that can always be changed once you have found your niche.

2. Buyer Account Set Up

   Now that you have your email, you will want to open accounts on the following: Alibaba, AliExpress, and DHGate. As you do this, be sure to check that your account info is always verified. This way, your account will instantly be ready to open up for business.

3. Google Spreadsheet

4. As you start a business, your primary goal is to stay organized. By starting a Google Sheet, you can save your accounts to the various web sites we just told you about. You will want to create tabs that are labeled "Credentials" or "Account Info." Please note that these are just suggestions. The information we provide you with are meant to be tools to help increase your rate of success. These tips are by no means vital for your business.

5. Amazon Seller's Account

6. Now that you are ready, it is time to go to Amazon and set up your seller account. To begin, we suggest setting up a free Individual Seller Plan. Later in the chapter, we will show you how to step up to FBA. For now, it is time to stick with the basics. As you do this, you will want to be sure that you are verifying your account information. Before we go over upgrading to FBA, we suggest understanding the

difference between the selling plans. This may sway your thoughts on joining FBA.

Individual Selling Plan

- $0.99 for each item that sells on Amazon
- Only one listing at a time
- Includes both online listing as well as the management of your orders
- Includes Seller Central tools to help with account functions

Professional Selling Plan

- Costs a Monthly Fee of $39.99
- Get multiple listings by using uploads and spreadsheets
- Includes reports and fees on your inventory and management of orders
- Includes access to the Amazon Marketplace Web Service, API functions, and daily reports on your store's performance.

7. Switching to Professional Plan

If you decide that FBA is the proper choice for your store, you can quickly switch your selling plan. To begin, you will want to click on the tab that says 'Seller Account.' Once you have done this, tap on the settings button and click 'Account Info.' Under this tab, it will ask you to click a button that says 'Modify

How to Sign Up on Amazon FBA to Get Started

Plan.' Once you are here, you will be able to upgrade your plan, and you are all set to go! The program processes immediately. It should be noted that you will be charged a $0.99 fee for any orders that you close. From this point on, you will be charged $39.99 a month as long as you keep the Professional plan.

8. Enrolling in FBA

9. Once you have experience selling items on Amazon, you may want to join FBA. At this time, you will want to go to amazon's FBA web page and click their 'Request Info' button. After filling out a contact form, Amazon will send you an invitation to join the program. Once this comes through, you will go through the sign-up process and be ready to go! For now, it is time to figure out what in the world you are going to sell!

Chapter Three:

How to Find a Profitable Product That Will Sell

Now that you are all set up with your FBA account, you are probably raring to go! The question is, where do you start? First, we suggest figuring out what your product is going to be. While some may suggest going after the "big niche" products, you may be surprised to find that you will most likely lose money this way. As a whole, there really is no "niche" that you can make a lot of money off; it is all about finding the proper product.

This stands especially true if you are an Amazon beginner. Instead of choosing multiple products, find one that you sell really well. You do not need a niche as of yet. If you do this, you are more likely to become overwhelmed by product and quitting. Obviously, this is something we want to avoid. When you find a specific product that you like, you will learn more about it and the demand for it. As this happens, you can try to branch out from there. Below, we will break down the steps to finding the best product for you.

❖ **Tip # 1: Lightweight Products**

 ➢ When you think about the cost of everything, you will want your product to be small and light. For FBA, the bigger your product, the more you will pay

How to Find a Profitable Product That Will Sell

> for shipping. If this happens, it just takes away from your profits. Before you choose a product, think smart. In the best interest of the seller, choose a product that is five pounds or less.

- Luckily, Amazon makes it pretty simple to figure out how much shipping costs. All you need to figure out is the whole weight of the box. This includes item, package, and the packaging inside. In order to figure this out, you will need to find your product first.

- The weight of the product will also come into play if you are having your items shipped from a third party. Let's say that your supplier is in China, and the items need to be sent to an Amazon warehouse. This is another area you can cut back on shipping costs, increasing your overall profit margin.

- As for fees with shipping, Amazon will charge $2 for a two-pound package. If you exceed this, the shipping rate also increases by $0.39. You will want to consider these fees when you choose your product.

- On a final note, the lighter and smaller your product is, the better. You should not be wasting your money on shipping and handling when you could invest that money somewhere else...like your pocket!

❖ Tip # 2: Understanding Average Product Sales

- While this will range depending on who you talk to, we have found that the most products sell between the $10 and $50 range. You would be surprised how many people shop due to their impulses to buy products. At the price range between these two numbers, the customer is less likely to do research before they purchase the item. If it is between $10 and $50, people most likely will not think twice about the choice as it isn't seen as much of a risk.

➢ Choosing a product in between this range will give you a lower barrier. This meaning that you can add more product quickly because people are buying it immediately. This way, there isn't product laying around. If it sells, you know you are getting the most bang for your buck at the end of the day. This also makes sure that you are getting your store started for less money. This is definitely the best option for beginners. Most of the time, those just starting out with online sales do not have a large budget to get started. By choosing a product in this range, it makes keeping the store affordable for both customer and retailer.

❖ Tip #3: Brand Names

➢ Beginners will struggle with this when they first start with Fulfilment by Amazon. If you think about it for a moment, why would you try to compete with the big names? While of course, it seems like a good idea, in theory, there is going to be a lot of competition. Instead, we suggest finding a product that has a weaker competition. This way, you will be able to sell more.

➢ You will want to begin by figuring out who your competition is in the first place. Once you have figured out your product that you are interested in, do a quick search for the product on Amazon. After looking at the first page, you will most likely come across big brands that have the product. If they have the exact product, we suggest finding something else. If you are a beginner, it is hard to play with the big dogs. That is until you build your brand. As you will be learning, we go over this later in the book.

➢ To increase your sales, try to compete against other no-name companies. Although it may take some extra effort and some more of your time than you would like to find a product, it will give you a higher chance of making sales as soon as possible. On top of this, it will not require a lot of marketing and much less competition.

❖ Tip #4: Understanding BSR

➢ So, what does BSR stand for in the Amazon world? BSR stands for Best Seller Ranking. This concept of ranking is going to be a key tool when you are deciding on a product to sell on Amazon. The BSR will be one of the best ways to measure how well a product is performing on the market. When it comes down to it, a lower BSR is going to be better. This is especially true for the products that are part of a large category. This meaning that a product with a BSR of 500 will be selling much better compared to one with a BSR of 10,000.

➢ When you choose a product, you are going to want to source. To do this successfully, you want your products inside of a certain category to have a BSR that is 5,000 or lower. If the products have a BSR of

5,000 or better, your odds of increasing your sales will also increase.

- If the product has a low ranking, this means that you will be granted the ability to sell more product. This is true as long as the existing products are already selling. As long as that number is low, you will know that there is plenty of money in this specific market. If you are a beginner, this is another fantastic tip to take with you when choosing your product.

❖ Tip #5: Pay Attention To Customer Reviews

- So, you think you have chosen the right product for you? Before you are certain, try to do some more research. If there are existing reviews on a similar product, how many are there? The more reviews there are, there is an increased chance that it will be harder to sell this product. You should note that there are thousands of products sold in a single day on Amazon. If there are a lot of reviews on the first page, this is a tell-tale sign that there will most likely be competition in this specific category.

- As a simple rule to follow, try to find a product that has 50 customer reviews or less. If there are even less, this will give you a better chance of selling the product. Building up your reviews is going to be important for your success. Remember that you are competing against others. The customer will most likely go for the product with more reviews. We will go over this in a later chapter.

> If you didn't think it was that important, note that one of the most popular Amazon search results comes from customer reviews. Clients care what other people think and what their experience is. This is something you will want to put some extra time and effort in for the betterment of your company.

❖ Tip #6: Keep It Simple

> When you are choosing your product, you will want to keep it as simple as possible. This way, there is less worry wondering if the product will be damaged while being shipped from point A to point B. This factor is not something you want to worry about, especially when shipping is not in your hands. Some great examples of a product like this would be cutting boards, yoga mats, or even a simple wallet. True, these are generic items, but they can be sourced and shipped from just about anywhere!

> By choosing a simpler product, this is less time you will be spending struggling with any defective goods. Most of the time, these are the products that will be cheaper to be made anyway. As you purchase your product, consider the following:

- Product should be durable
- Product should not contain electronic parts
- Product should not contain moving parts
- Product should be able to be used with a manual
- Product should have one job

Amazon FBA for Beginners

- Product should be lightweight and small

❖ Tip #6: Think Better, Think Smarter

➢ You may have chosen a product because it isn't represented well. When you look at your competition, are the listings as optimized to the best of their ability? There are a few aspects you want to take into account when setting up your listing. See if your competition has done the following:

- Is it missing important information?
- Are there low bullet points of information?
- Is there a non-descriptive title?
- Are the pictures awful?
- Are there a small number of images?

➢ Note that the items from above are super important to customers. If this is something your competition is missing, jump on the item! As you have the ability to improve your listings, it will be that much easier to climb the ranks and maybe even make your way to the front page!

❖ Tip # 7: Buy Low and Sell High

➢ When choosing your product, you will want to realize that you will need to manage every number to keep up with your profit margin. The key to having a successful business is to buy low and then sell the product at a higher price. For a number to follow, try to source your product for 25% less compared to the sale on Amazon.

➢ The most convenient way to do this is to find a product that is from a foreign marketplace. This is where AliBaba will come into play. Within the list of these manufacturers and suppliers, you are more likely to find a product to purchase for cheap. For example, on the AliBaba website, it will tell you how much the item will cost to have it made. So, if your product is made for $5 and it will sell for $20 on Amazon, you will be able to make a good profit. You want to make sure it is less than the selling price because you have other fees you need to cover.

➢ If you are a beginner, we suggest sticking to a 75% profit margin. This will most likely be enough to cover all of the costs that comes with selling product on Amazon. Your goal is to make a profit margin including everything that comes with online sales. When done right, you will see more income than outcome!

❖ Tip #8: Made in China

➢ Up to this point, you have heard of AliBaba multiple times. When it comes to choosing a product, you want it to be semi-easy to find on Amazon. If it isn't, it will probably be difficult to make overseas. If this is what is happening, you are most likely looking at a hefty price to have the goods made in the first place.

➢ As you do the research for your product, you will want to pay attention to how many companies manufacture the item you are looking for. Are there multiple suppliers? If there are, this is an excellent sign. This way, you can compete on price so you can get the lowest possible offer. It is also a very good idea to have a backup plan in case a company decides to stop selling your product. It is always to have multiple plans to make online sales foolproof!

❖ Tip #9: Understanding Keywords

- Up to this point, you probably have an item that has made it through the checklist. As you continue through your research of finding keywords, you will want to use a tool known as "MerchantWords." With this tool, you can look for the keywords that your customers are using to find their product. By knowing what the client is looking for, you can increase your sales by being in the know.

- As a good guideline, try to find a product that gets a minimum of 100,000 searches within one month. You will want to try to use keywords that incorporate the primary product. If this doesn't come up, try to find a combination of a few different keyword sets. You will be surprised how different the search results will change when you change a few words!

❖ Tip #10: Explore Other Outlets

- It is always a possibility that Amazon isn't the best option for your product. There are other marketplaces on the internet including eBay and Etsy. You will want to do some research on these other outlets to see what is selling on the other sites. Check out if the product is similar to yours? If there is, this is a good sign that there is a market for your product. True, you are competing with other outlets, but with FBA, you have a step up and a wider audience.

❖ Tip # 11: Seasonal Seller

- ➢ If you are a beginner, this concept may be a tad advance for you. Some seasonal products sell well and make good for a quick turnaround, but this isn't a product you will be able to sell all year. If you are just starting out, we suggest choosing a product that will sell all year long. If making profit for a few months is all you are looking for, seasonal will be a great idea. It's a little work for a short time and a quick outcome.

❖ Tip #12: Recurring Purchases

- ➢ When you are searching for a product, consider one that encourages multiple purchases. This way, you will have the same customers buying multiple times in a year. With this concept, you will spend less on shipping items to Amazon, and you will increase your profit margin! However, with this concept, it is of the utmost importance that you treat your customer right. If you want a recurring purchase, the first one needs to go smoothly. This way, you will receive a high review rating. Overall, recurring purchases means less work and more money in the long run.

- ❖ **Advanced Tip #13: Consider Expanding**

  ➢ This tip is for the sellers who have found the perfect product. While we do not suggest selling many items, it could be a good idea to find a product that has the ability to expand at a later time. For this, you will want to find a product and then related products that customers have bought at well. This will increase your chances of the same customer coming back for a second purchase. If the trust the seller, they are more likely to return for another purchase.

  ➢ If you only want to sell a single product as a beginner, this is perfectly fine. This advance tip is only necessary for those who want to build a brand for themselves. After all, you will most likely want to give yourself the room to grow into your future. As you begin to build a brand for yourself, you will increase your profits in the future as well.

Chapter Four:

How to Ship and Manage Inventory

After the third chapter, you may have found your perfect product to start your store with. So, how do you ship it? While of course, Amazon does a majority of the work, do not allow this factor to give you a fake sense of security. Although FBA will take care of a lot of the side work such as shipping and customer service, you cannot just set the job aside and forget about it! Before we go into how to ship your items as well as manage your inventory, we have a few tips on what not to do. This way, you can stay organized and on top of everything that happens with your business.

1. **You Have to Manage Your Inventory**

    For some beginners, this is a very hard concept to grasp. Through FBA, it is easy to get on auto-pilot with your store. This being because, through Amazon, you will no longer have the physical product in front of you. On top of this, you should note that there is a limit to how many items you can ship to certain Amazon centers.

    With this being said, Fulfilment By Amazon is a very fluid market. What we mean by this is that there is a grand velocity of product sales. On a daily basis, competitors are entering the same market as you, and others who are leaving. As this happens, the market will respond accordingly, and you need to be on top of this. This stands especially true for those retailers who want to grow as the business grows. You will need to understand what you want to sell, how much you want to sell, how much you need to restock an item and when to sell this item. Yes, you could just list and leave, but you will not make the most of your profits this way.

2. **Keeping Profits Organized**

As you now know, the market is going to fluctuate due to a number of reasons. For most sellers, they price their product according to the competition. Unfortunately, some sellers need to raise their prices to match their competitors, including the shipping cost of the item. For most people, it has been found that they need to leverage Amazon's infrastructure in order to gain the most profit.

Your main goal is to keep track of your profits. In general, FBA margins tend to trend on the tighter side. This is from Amazon's fees. For most people, this drives down the selling prices on most of their products. If you are organized, you will have no issue keeping tabs on these margins. By doing so, you'll keep track of your profits and make sure that online sales are worth the work.

3. **Issues with Overstocking and Understocking**

4. This is one of the main issues sellers on Amazon have. The goal is to find the sweet spot with your product. While you do not want to under-stock in the case of a

spike in customers, you certainly never want to have product lying around because you overstocked your store. If you overstock, you will be charged a warehousing fee. When you are charged a fee, it will take away from the profit of your product. However, if you understock, you will lose sales and most likely will not have customers return because the product was not there when you wanted it. By being aware of the trends on Amazon, you will be able to find a comfortable product number to keep everyone happy.

5. **Do Not Fall Invisible Or Overload Yourself**

6. True, FBA can simplify your job of creating online sales, but it will increase your demand in other areas. As the market changes, you will need to find a way to keep track of the information on the market that is constantly changing. Your main goal should be to remain detailed with your product. However, there is a fine line. If you have an excessive amount of data, you could produce a paralysis of your analysis. If this happens, you could change to a passive approach when you manage your own inventory.

7. While it is ok to deal with these issues yourself, please note that there are programs out there to help you out with the other aspects of running an online business such as your visibility factor. Try out Amazon Selling Coach or even The Inventory Health Report. These are basically spreadsheets that help you organize the market, your information, and other purposes of FBA.

8. **Accidental Shipping Errors**

9. When your product is being managed by others, there is bound to be errors. As obnoxious as it is, the error is inevitable. If you are on top of the shipping, you can avoid mistakes as much as possible. When you are well organized with your data, you will be able to identify the mistake and minimize the impact on the customer. You will want to make sure you make the proper adjustments as quickly as possible. Here are a few ways you can go about staying organized:

   - Create visual tools to monitor your product

   - Create POs to help you check data i.e.: shipping weight

   - Make processes automatic to lessen data-entry errors

   - Use tools to add, delete, or change shipping information

How to Send FBA Inventory

Now that you have your product and you understand what you need to do to run a tight ship, it is time to learn how to send your inventory to Amazon in the first place. The first step for shipping you will want to do is create your own shipping plan. This plan will include products you plan on sending to the Amazon fulfillment center in list form.

On Amazon, there is a very simple shipment creation tool. Through this, you can select the products you want to send, along with the quantity of each item. Once you have selected your items, you will want to choose your shipping method and decide if you would like to label and prepare the item yourself. If not, you can have Amazon do all of the work for a fee. Later in the book, we will give you a comprehensive guide to all fees Amazon tacks on. With the shipment tool, Amazon will provide you with tips and tricks on how to prepare your items. It will also give you the shipping labels and packing slip you need to provide with your package. After you select your plan for shipping, you can ship the items to the fulfillment centers, and you are on your way! Below, we will provide a step by step guide on how to add your inventory into your shipping plan if you have never done it before.

1. The first step, you will want to sign into your Amazon account. Once you are in, click on the 'Manage Inventory' page.

2. When you are here, you can choose your items that require shipping. When you have chosen everything, go ahead and click "Send Inventory." This will be located under your Action on Selected menu.

3. Once you are on the "Send Inventory" page, you will have to choose either

4. a) Create New Shipping Plan

5. b) Add to Existing Shipping Plan

6. Once you choose between creating a new shipping plan or adding to an existing one, you will be prompted to confirm your address. You must provide the address where your shipment is going to be picked up. If you do go with a supplier, be sure to provide the address of their warehouse. Otherwise, your home business or house address will be fine.

7. Next, you will be asked to confirm your package type. You will either have an Individual Product or Case-packed products. The individual products are your single items whereas case-packed products are usually the same item that is packaged by the maker.

8. Last, click continues to shipping plan, and you are ready to go!

How To Manage Your Orders

As you probably realize, Amazon has tried to make everything as simple as possible. On their website, you will find that their Manage Orders tools are a fantastic way to stay organized with all of your sales. Through here, you will be able to view your orders and do Advanced searches to find a specific order when you need. You will be able to find the listing in a number of ways:

1. Order Date

2. If you know when the order was submitted, you can organize your shipments by date and time. For some people, this is the best way to stay organized

3. Order Details

4. If you choose to organize by order details, you get a number of different information. This will include: the order id, the quantity ordered, the product title, the buyer, the sales channel, a fulfillment method, the billing country, the ASIN, and the SKU.

5. Shipping Type

6. Status

7. As a seller, the shipping status is something you will want to pay attention to. Please note that sellers will be required to confirm any shipments with Amazon. This must be done within 30 days or else Amazon cancels the order, and the seller will not be paid. In most cases, the seller will be warned a week before the cut-off, but this is something you really must be aware of. The statuses include Unshipped, Shipped, Pending, Cancelled, or Refund Applied.

8. Action

9. Finally, your orders can be managed through the following actions: Refund order, Cancel order, Confirm Shipment, Print Packing Slip, Edit Shipment

How to Import Items From Overseas

If you want to create the least work possible for the most money, you should be considering buying in bulk from overseas. There are intelligent ways to go about this. For example, if you ship overseas, this will take longer, but it will be cheaper. If you ship through the air, it is faster and easier, but it will cost you. This factor will change depending on how much you want to invest in your new business. Sure, it can be intimidating to get started, but once you understand the operation, you will be glad you learned. Below, we will provide a guide on how we feel is the easiest way to process product from overseas.

Step One: Get the Sample

This step is crucial for your success on Amazon. You should be aware that getting a sample will cost you, but it will be worth it in the end. Instead of thinking of it as an upfront cost, look at it as an investment into the future of your product. As you choose your items, you will want to make sure you have the highest quality. As a beginner, you want to find a manufacturer you can trust.

Step Two: Communication is Key

When you are choosing a supplier, communication will be very important for your long-term relationship. First, you will want to make sure they respond quickly. If they are quick, check out their English skills. Communication will be key to your organization. If you cannot understand each other, the language barrier could create errors in the future.

Step Three: Getting a Working Relationship

Much like with any relationship, it is about giving and taking. While you do want to give this person your business, you will also want to protect yourself from any mishaps. By remaining professional and serious, you will be able to build a relationship with your choosing. Remember that your first steps are to gain access to clear communication and study their product before deciding to work with anyone.

Step Four: Understanding the Process

When you develop a positive relationship, it is time to work out the details. You will want to ask questions such as quality standards, policies, fees, and manufacturing time. As you build your business, you will know what you want and what you don't want. As we stated earlier, we suggest sticking with one product at once. This way, you will get to know the product, the supplier, and if it will work for you in the long run.

Chapter Five:

How to Market for Improving Sales

Now that you've got the product and the ability to ship it, where do you go from here? You have to admit; you will not be making any sales if people aren't viewing your product! As we mentioned earlier, FBA will open a broader audience for your product, but sometimes, that is not enough. Instead, it is time to take the future of your product into your own hands. To follow, we will be providing you with some tricks to enhance your market skills and get your product viewed by more people. The more it's seen, the more it will sell.

Improve SEO

One of your first steps is to understand the keywords people are using in their listings. This is especially important for your title. This is a tactic that many SEA agencies use in order to improve their Google ranking. If you weren't already aware, your title can have up to 500 characters. This means that you have a pretty big title to ensure you include as many keywords as possible. When coming up with the title, include the color, the material, the product line, quantity, brand and a short description if possible.

If you aren't good with words, there's an app for that. Try using Amazon Keyword Tool. Through this service, the tool will find the popular keywords that could help you out. It makes sure the words are best fit for your product and can place them into a Planner Tool. Once it is placed here, you are granted the ability to search the volume the keywords have access to. Knowledge and organization will be your best friend during this process. Yes, it will take some extra work, but you should do whatever it takes to get your item sold.

FREE PRODUCT

You may be shaking your head, saying absolutely no way, but hear us out. By giving away free product, it could help your prospects in the future. Yes, in a short term standpoint, it probably isn't a good idea, but this will help you get reviews. As you will be learning a bit later, reviews are crucial for your success. If you want, offer a customer a 99% discount code. The catch being that they need to leave you a review. The more reviews you get, the better your ranking on Amazon searches. If you do this, you could also gain customers for life.

If you have been doing Amazon for a while, this is also a great way to get rid of any inventory that has been sitting around. It will help generate customers, and they will more likely turn to you in the future. Try to link your store to Amazon Seller Central to identify items given by other channels. With this extra step, you will learn how to manage your inventory in a more productive manner.

Learn How to Advertise

Amazon has a newer feature known as Amazon Sponsored Products. If you are a beginner, this could be the perfect avenue for you. By choosing a product that is sponsored by Amazon, the product will be shown directly under the search results. If it is not here, it will be on the details page or on the right-hand side. As of now, this isn't a big avenue, but Amazon has stated that they are hoping to expand the feature. The goal is to make the advertisements more visible for the shoppers. Currently, Amazon offers free credit if you take this avenue. The real question you should be asking yourself is what you have got to lose in choosing this avenue?

Think Outside The Market Box

Just because you are on Amazon, does not mean that you only need to advertise on this one website. Try to think outside of the marketing box. We suggest trying outlets including direct calls or emails to stay in touch with customers. Another great way to gain a bigger audience is to start a blog or write a few articles. Through this, you can target any niche you desire.

Another great option to write articles is to choose a specific outlet. There are sites out there like Go Articles, Hubpages, and even Isnare. When you write your articles, this will give you the ability to share a link to your store, present coupons, and notify the public when you have one-time promotions. You would be surprised how many people will jump on an opportunity to have free shopping or buy one, get one free promotion.

It's All About the Discounts

Just as people like a good deal, they love discounts even more. When you have a discount on your items, it is a fantastic way to motivate buyers. If they see your item as a good deal, they won't second guess their decision. Due to the fact they had a good experience with your store (hopefully) this can help build a long-term relationship.

If you create a discount on your item, this could also increase your visibility. It will increase your chances of ending up on the home page of Amazon under "New & Noteworthy" or even "Hot Deals." Increasing your exposure is incredibly important. The more traffic you receive, you will increase your chances of selling your product. If they buy it once at a discount, they may buy it a second time at full price.

Keep Up With the Competition

This is a fantastic tip to have when entering the world of Amazon Prime. For some sellers, they avoid Amazon due to the competition. The question is, are you afraid of a little challenge? Some may find it enjoyable to be in the game. The game is to win the buy box. The buy box is in charge of the button the shopper will click to add the purchase to their cart. If you are organized and monitor your prices compared to the competitor, you are in the win. Even if you just make your item a penny cheaper than your competition, this small change could make you the winner. The only matter is that this will take up time. However, the time will be worth it when your product is chosen over a similar competition.

Chapter Six:

How to Get Stellar Reviews Every Time

If you haven't realized at this point, your reviews on Amazon are going to be very important for the success of your business. Luckily, whether you are new or an Amazon pro, there are ways to improve your reviews and keep them stellar. The more reviews you have, the better. If they are five-star reviews, this is even better.

As we mentioned earlier, reviews will help you win the Buy Box. When you win the buy box, this will improve your feedback score and show all of your customers that you have a trustworthy reputation. It should be noted that anywhere between 70-80% of Amazon sales are made through the Buy Box. This is why it is so critical. Below, we will list some of the ways to keep a 100% positive feedback.

Tip #1: Be Honest About Condition

If you are on the edge, we suggest that you always round down. For instance, say you have a book you want to sell, and you think it's either good condition or very good condition. We suggest sticking to good condition. With customers, you never know how picky they are going to be. If it isn't as they were expecting, you will get a negative review. In this case, it is important you play the game safe and round down. Plus, it can only go up from there. If they think it is in better condition compared to what they were expecting, this could lead to a positive rating anyway!

Tip #2: Act ASAP

Negative feedbacks are bound to happen; it is just part of the game. The important factor is where you can make the difference. If you receive unfair negative feedbacks, a bad product review, or a price complaint, you will want to act as soon as you can. You will be able to do this by opening up a ticket with your Seller Support. Once you have done this, you can ask Amazon to remove the feedback. If you weren't aware, it is against the policy of Amazon to leave negative feedback due to the product or price. The key to this issue is to limit the number of words you use. Sellers have found that if you have a bulky message, complaining about the injustice of the customer, they will more than likely deny your removal request. Communication is key. If they deny your request, you can always open another ticket. Eventually, a staff member will side with you and remove the negative feedback. Remember always to be nice!

Tip #3: Admit When You Are Wrong

Of course, there will always be the cases when you are absolutely in the wrong. It could be a condition issue or anything else that is a legitimate reason to complain. At these moments, you need to be able to admit when you are in the wrong, but this does not mean end game. If you fall into this issue, you still need to act quickly, but now your fate is in the customer's hands. When answering, try to reach out to your buyer. You will want to communicate with them and express how sorry you are for your mistake. Next, you will want to ask if there is anything you can do to make it up and that customer

Amazon FBA for Beginners

satisfaction is very important to you. Some sellers have even been known to offer gift cards to make up for the mistake. More than likely, a customer will appreciate the extra effort. If they do accept your offer, throw in that your feedback score is important and ask them to consider kindly removing their negative feedback. When you do this, it would be beneficial to provide instructions on how to change the feedback score.

If you do offer a gift card, be careful with your words! It is against Amazon policy to offer gift cards to bribe buyers to remove their feedback. You will want to avoid putting these two requests in the same message, let along the same sentence. Unless you are working with a stubborn customer, they will most likely change their feedback.

Tip #4: Check Over the Product

When you are sending your product into Amazon, be honest with yourself about the condition of the item you are selling. You should realize that not everyone will carry the same values as you when buying a product. What is a very good condition to you may be an ok condition to another. It is better to have higher standards than most. Even if you feel you are being honest about the product, try to get another view of the product. This is just one easy way to avoid a negative review due to a standard difference. When describing your product, you will want to provide as much information as you can. This way, you will avoid any false expectations from both sides of the party.

Tip #5: Always Follow Up

Most customers will appreciate the extra step coming from the seller. Most customers will receive a generic from Amazon asking for feedback once they have purchased an item. You can take the extra effort and write a personalized request. If you are looking for a good time, try to send the message once they have received their product. This way, the memory of receiving the package is fresh in their head. Luckily, some tools and websites can send request emails automatically. This way, you are spending less time while still improving your customer satisfaction.

Tip #6: Follow the Competition

Following your competition can be done fairly easy. If you are on Amazon, you will want to search for items on your product page. There is a nifty little link labeled "Customers Who Viewed This Item Also Viewed," and "Customers Who Bought This Item Also Bought." Most of the time, it will lead you right to your competitors. As you go through their items, check out what people are saying in their reviews. This way, you can note what they are excelling at, and what they could improve on. As you do your research, you will continue to learn what you can incorporate into your own listings.

Tip #7: Amazon and Social Media

If you are on Amazon, you may want to consider starting a newsletter. By doing this, you will be able to keep in touch with your customer base. For most people, they will probably appreciate the extra effort. If you are not a newsletter type, a Facebook page where people could follow you would be perfect. On these two mediums, you could ask your customers for reviews. If they follow you, they have most likely already bought an item from you. While other companies may discourage asking for reviews, Amazon users do not seem to care.

Tip #8: Use Your Tools

Sometimes, there is just not enough time in the day. If you ever feel this way, there are tools on the internet to help you with small annoyances such as leaving feedback. It is known as the Feedback Genius. Sellers have stated that their positive feedback doubled since using the Feedback Genius. What is basically does is connect to your account on Amazon and sends your customers an automated email. First, they receive an email stating when the package is going to be delivered. Once it is delivered, another automatic message goes out asking the customers about their satisfaction with their order and that you will fix any issues as soon as possible. By being on top of the issue, a customer is more likely to turn to you first rather than just angrily leaving a negative review. If the customer forgot to leave a review, the Genius will send a separate reminder about leaving feedback.

One of the most convenient features of the Genius is the text updates. For example, if you set the feedback setting to texting if you receive a feedback score of 3 or lower, the Genius will notify you as soon as possible. The sooner you know, the sooner you will be able to act on the issue. Some of us cannot be attached to our computers at all times. By having this process, you will be able to work in real time in the event of receiving a negative feedback. Simply remember the policies of Amazon, and you are on the road to success.

Chapter Seven:

Learning About Fees and Tax Issues

As with any good business, there are going to be fees. When you weight the fees with your success as a seller, they will most likely be worth it. You should note that as you work on a market online, it has the ability to change. Starting February of 2017, the fees for FBA are making a change. If you haven't started your business yet, this is probably a good thing to consider as there are many changes Amazon is making within the next year.

1. **Elimination of No Fee Fulfillment**

2. Starting in February, fees will always be based on the size of the product. Before that, there was a discount for normal sized items that could sell for more than $300. This will not be the case anymore.

3. **Increased Fee for Any Media Products**

4. Normally, the fee for media products were lower compared to Non-media products. Now, they are going to be consolidated into one standard size. This meaning that the fee price of media products will increase to match the latter.

Learning About Fees and Tax Issues

5. **Seller Shipment Requirements Changes**

6. As a seller, you will now be asked more often how you want to send items as you create your shipping plan. You still have the option to send to multiple destinations. Now, a per-item service fee is going to apply if you use any Inventory Placement Services.

7. **Monthly Inventory Fee**

8. Starting in October of 2017, there is going to me a monthly storage fee. This will increase even more if you have oversized items. As we stated earlier, we will be giving you the exact numbers a little later in this chapter.

9. **Q4 Fulfilment Fees**

10. Also starting in October of 2017, Amazon will be reducing their shipment fees. This change will be consistent through both November and December. This will give users the chance to reduce their storage space to lower their FBA fees altogether.

11. **Consolidation of Any FBA Fees**

12. Starting in February of 2017, all of the fees for Packing and Handling are going to be consolidated to one fee. The hope is that this makes it a bit easier on the sellers. Now, it is time to get down to the real numbers. This way, you can make a choice depending on your life and business, if selling on FBA will be worth it.

Amazon FBA for Beginners

Fulfilment Fees for FBA starting February 22, 2017 (Standard Non-Media & Media Products)

	Small (1 Pound or Less)	Large (1 Pound or Less)	Large (1 to 2 Pounds)	Large (2 Pounds or More)
January-September	$2.41	$2.99	$4.18	$4.18 $0.39 per pound if over 2 Pounds
October-December	$2.39	$2.88	$3.96	$3.96 $0.39 per pound if over 2 Pounds

Fulfilment Fees for FBA starting February 22, 2017 (Oversized Products)

	Small	Medium	Large	Special
January-September	$6.85 $0.39 per pound if over 2 Pounds	$9.20 $0.39 per pound if over 2 Pounds	$75.06 $0.80 per pound when over 90 pounds	$138.08 $0.92 per pound when over 90 pounds
October-December	$6.69 $0.35 per pound if over 2 Pounds	$8.73 $0.35 per pound if over 2 Pounds	$69.50 $0.76 per pound when over 90 pounds	$131.44 $0.88 per pound when over 90 pounds

Learning About Fees and Tax Issues

Monthly Storage Fees

When Amazon first started, they had plenty of room to grow. However, with so many sellers, they need to come up with a way to control inventory. This is where the monthly fees will come into play. There will be a fee for a standard-size product between the months of January and September. Please note that these fees will change October and will continue through November and December. Check the fees out below.

	Standard-Size	Oversize
January-September	$.64 for each cubic foot	$.43 for each cubic foot
October-December	$2.35 for each cubic foot	$1.15 for each cubic foot

Product Placement Fees

As we stated earlier, beginning in July of 2017, Amazon will begin to ask more often if you want to send your items to other destinations. This will happen as you create your shipping plan. You will still need to either follow the plan of Amazon or choose to use an Inventory Placement. Through this option, you will be able to ship to a fewer number of destinations. Please note that there will be a fee is you use the Inventory Placement Service. It will change depending on the number of destinations

Placement Service Fees starting July 19, 2017 (Standard Product Size)

Amazon Ship Destinations as Recommended	Three	Two	One
Three	Free	$.10 and $.10 per pound if over 2 pounds	$.30 and $.10 per pound if over 2 pounds
Two	Free	Free	$.20 and $.10 per pound if over 2 pounds
One	Free	Free	Free

Learning About Fees and Tax Issues

Placement Service Fees starting July 19, 2017 (Oversized)

Amazon Ship Destinations as Recommended	Three	Two	One
Three	Free	$.50 and $.20 per pound if over 5 pounds	$1.65 and $.20 per pound if over 5 pounds
Two	Free	Free	$.70 and $.20 per pound if over 5 pounds
One	Free	Free	Free

Understanding FBA Taxes

While taxes are tricky on their own anyway, they can become quite confusing if you are not aware of what you are doing on Fulfilment By Amazon. The trick here is to know that you will most likely only owe taxes depending on where your product is placed. For those of you using Amazon as storage, this will include any state that your product is being stored. What you first must know is where your products are so you can determine in which states you will owe your taxes. So, how do you do this? We will explain.

What is Sales Tax?

If you weren't already aware, every state minus New Hampshire, Montana, Oregon or Delaware have sales tax. There are also other cities and counties which charge a sales tax that will later be placed on the state sales tax. At first, sales tax can seem like a disappointment. It should be noted that these are the funds that help out your fire departments, schools, and the roads you travel on every day.

Sales Tax and Amazon FBA

As we stated earlier, if you are using Amazon FBA, your products are most likely stored in various states in the different fulfillment centers. For sellers, this is one of the main benefits of Amazon FBA. It will lower shipping costs, make shipping quicker, and can even save the planet by reducing your carbon footprint. But, with most benefits, comes the downfall and this is where sales tax may come into play.

Here is where it can get a bit tricky. When your product is being stored in a state, you must collect state taxes on any products that are sold in the same state. When your product is physically present in a state, this will trigger nexus. Now, what is nexus? Basically, it means that you have sales tax liability in that area. When you have nexus in a particular state, you will have to charge sales tax when a customer purchases your item.

Your first step to deciding where you will owe taxes is to figure out where your product is stored in the first place. Luckily, some tools can help you do this. In particular, try out Taxify. There is a free trial, and it connects directly to your Amazon store! Through this application, it can show you the states your product is in and if you owe taxes.

Learning About Fees and Tax Issues

How to Get Your Sales Tax License

Now that you have found out where your product is, it is time to register for your sales tax license. You will be required to do this in each state your product is physically present. This is very important because if you don't, you will be breaking the law. If you fail to collect state taxes, you will be charged expensive penalties and fines.

In order to apply for the tax license, you will be required to research each state tax authority for each of the states. For most states, it is pretty easy to apply for the license online. Please note that they may come with a fee. If you have any questions, you can probably call the authority and ask for help.

Collecting Taxes on Amazon

Luckily, Amazon makes this process pretty easy. When you set up your professional store, you can collect your taxes on any sales that are applicable. Here is a step-by-step guide to make sure you are doing it the right way.

1. First, you will want to sign into your account. Once you are on your Seller page, go ahead and click on your settings tab followed by the Tax Settings.

2. Now, you will read something that says "Welcome to The Tax Manager." Here, you will want to click on the third link that says "View/Edit Your Taxes."

3. Once here, scroll down to the segment that says "Choose Shipping & Handling Tax Settings."

4. You will want to check the second box that says "Enroll is Amazon Tax Exemption Program."

5. Now, you will want to go through the list and check the states where you owe taxes (Where the product is stored) and where you have your sales tax license.

6. When this is done, Amazon will collect the taxes. Please note that you will still need to submit these taxes to the government as that is not Amazon's job.

As a special note, we warn you never to check the box that says to collect taxes in every state. If you do this, you will be required to get a sales tax license in every state. This could be a huge headache at the end of the day. This is why we recommend only sticking with the states your product is in.

Conclusion

Congratulations! At this point in our book, you are probably an Amazon FBA expert! If you aren't feeling particularly confident in an area, feel free to go back and review the tools we have provided you with. From learning about FBA to finding the perfect product to sell, and even going over the difficult sales tax situation, we have got you covered. Hopefully, at this point, you are ready to make the leap and start your own FBA business. In case you need a reminder, here is a quick Beneficial list for you to consider:

Pros of Amazon FBA:

- **Amazon Prime**

    - Remember Amazon will bring you a wider audience to view your product. This stands especially true for those who subscribe to Prime. These users are 150% more likely to buy more expensive items, more often. This will open a whole new world for your product, giving you the chance to increase your sales without having to do anything!

- **Amazing Customer Service**

    - With Amazon, everything is going to be off your plate. They will pick it up, pack it up, and send it out. Note that quick shipping will lead to a happy customer. If they aren't, Amazon will take care of that too! On top of that, you will not have a bunch of product laying around your home. They will be kept neat and organized in Amazon's very own fulfillment centers.

➢ **More!**

- While of course this is never guaranteed, as it will come with some hard work, some sellers on Amazon have reported a 20% increase in sales when they started with Amazon FBA. For some, they even doubled their original sales volume. This may be due to strategy or Prime. Either way, it is worth a shot!

➢ **Price Increase**

- It has been found that when you get Prime members purchasing your item, they are more likely to pay more as long as they get the free shipping. In the modern age, it is all about the added convenience at the end of the day.

➢ **The Buy Box**

- We kid you not when we express how important the Buy Box is. If you are using FBA, you have a higher chance of getting the Buy Box. It has been noted that even with a price of 2-10% higher compared to your competitor, you could still get the buy box. This is because your shipping is already calculated into your price. This will be very valuable to your customer. When they click the buy box, you make more money!

Now that you are an expert, it is time to send you on your way. We hope we have provided you with enough tools to get you started. Remember that it will take some hard work, but at the end of the day when you are working at home in your pajamas, it will be worth it!

www.ingramcontent.com/pod-product-compliance
Lightning Source LLC
Chambersburg PA
CBHW061221180526
45170CB00003B/1096